Dear Parent:

Buckle up! You are about to join your child on a very exciting journey. The destination? Independent reading!

Road to Reading will help you and your child get there. The program offers books at five levels, or Miles, that accompany children from their first attempts at reading to successfully reading on their own. Each Mile is paved with engaging stories and delightful artwork.

Getting Started
For children who know the alphabet and are eager to begin reading
• easy words • fun rhythms • big type • picture clues

Reading With Help
For children who recognize some words and sound out others with help
• short sentences • pattern stories • simple plotlines

Reading On Your Own
For children who are ready to read easy stories by themselves
• longer sentences • more complex plotlines • easy dialogue

First Chapter Books
For children who want to take the plunge into chapter books
• bite-size chapters • short paragraphs • full-color art

Chapter Books
For children who are comfortable reading independently
• longer chapters • occasional black-and-white illustrations

There's no need to hurry through the Miles. Road to Reading is designed without age or grade levels. Children can progress at their own speed, developing confidence and pride in their reading ability no matter what their age or grade.

So sit back and enjoy the ride—every Mile of the way!

To Geraldine & Edgar

Library of Congress Cataloging-in-Publication Data
Mayer, Mercer.
Little Critter's the best present / Mercer Mayer.
   p.   cm. — (Road to reading. Mile 2)
Originally published as Little Critter's Little Sister's Birthday and adapted from
Mercer Mayer's "Little Critter's Little Sister's Birthday" in Little Critter's Read-It-
Yourself Storybook: Six Funny Easy-to-Read Stories.
Summary: Little Critter helps Mom and Dad prepare a surprise birthday party for his
little sister.
ISBN 0-307-46215-3 (GB)—ISBN 0-307-26215-4 (pbk.)
[1. Birthdays—Fiction. 2. Parties—Fiction. 3. Brothers and sisters—Fiction.] I. Title:
Best present. II. Title. III. Series.

PZ7.M462 Lcp 2000
[E]—dc21   99-089570

A GOLDEN BOOK • New York
Golden Books Publishing Company, Inc. New York, New York 10106

ISBN: 0-307-26215-4 (pbk)   A MM
ISBN: 0-307-46215-3 (GB)

LITTLE CRITTER'S®
THE BEST PRESENT

BY
MERCER MAYER

It's my little sister's birthday.
We are giving her a party.
She doesn't know that.

5

Dad and I are going shopping.

My little sister wants to go, too.

But she has to stay home.

We are going to get
her birthday present.
She doesn't know that.

Dad and I drive to the mall.
We go to the toy store.

This would be
a good present.

Or this.

But this is the best present.
For my little sister, I mean.

We go home.

I put the present

in a box.

I get dressed.

The doorbell rings.
Surprise!

There are all of my
little sister's friends.

There are a lot of presents.

There are a lot of friends.

We go outside to play games.

We have a bag race.

We have an egg race, too.

Then we go inside.

We play more games.

It's time to eat.

Mom brings out
the birthday cake.

My little sister makes a wish.
She blows out all the candles.

Mom cuts the cake.

There's a lot of cake.

There's a piece
for everyone.

There's ice cream, too.

Now it's time
to open the presents.

My little sister
opens my present.

"Look at this!"
she cries.

She says it's
the best present.

I knew that!